PILATES

THE AUTHENTIC WAY

HINKLER
BOOKS

Box and book cover design: Hinkler Design Studio

Art Director: Karen Moores

Photograper: UB Photo

Editor: Fiona Staum

Clothing supplied by Yes Brasil

First published in this format 2006
by Hinkler Books Pty Ltd
45–55 Fairchild Street
Heatherton Victoria 3202 Australia
www.hinklerbooks.com

© Hinkler Books Pty Ltd 2003

2 4 6 8 10 9 7 5 3
07 09 11 10 08

Printed and bound in China

ISBN-10: 1 7418 1038 8
ISBN-13: 978 1 7418 1038 7

CONTENTS

INTRODUCTION

What is the Pilates Method?

The Pilates Method of body conditioning is a well-known mind-body exercise system that has a successful record of creating healthy, balanced bodies over the last 80 years.

Joseph H Pilates designed a system of exercises which combine stretching and strengthening, using apparatuses with spring resistance and mat exercises. He described it as 'contrology' or 'the art of control' which encompasses six principles of centring, concentration, control, precision, breathing and flowing movement.

The mat work has proven so popular because it can be done anywhere, and as a result of consistent practice, you will gain increased strength in the powerhouse and enjoy the following benefits:

- Lengthened muscles
- Improved posture
- Prevention and healing of injuries
- Improved flexibility
- A fun workout
- Enhanced energy and rejuvenation

The Pilates Method is a form of body conditioning that continues to challenge you and, as you get stronger, is a progressive form of exercise, that keeps you intrigued. There are 34 exercises in total on the mat, but remember, try not to add too many new exercises at once – try to perform each exercise with quality and control.

Pilates the Authentic Way is based on the original system of exercises as taught by Joseph H Pilates. Dina Matty and Keft Burdell were trained by master instructors, Romana Kryzanowska and Cynthia Lochard who are a source of inspiration as they teach with brilliance, humour and tireless devotion to keep the Pilates Method pure and in its original form.

THE PILATES PRINCIPLES

6 POWER-PACKED PILATES PRINCIPLES

1. Concentration

Pilates is a mind-body connection. Focus on all the movements you perform in each exercise and the area of the body working. Visualisations throughout the workout help connect the mind and body.

2. Control

Joseph Pilates called his method the 'art of contrology'. Concentration and control are needed to perform on the mat, to avoid injury and achieve the ultimate goal of each exercise.

3. Centring

All the work on the Pilates mat comes from your centre, which we call the powerhouse. The energy begins from your powerhouse and then flows to your extremities.

4. Precision

Precision is the key to enable you to reach perfect form in each exercise. Each individual movement should be performed with precision.

5. Breath

Control of the body works with breath. On inhalation we fill the body with oxygen to revitalise and on exhalation you empty the lungs of stale air. This enables us to perform with quality of movement.

6. Flow

The sequence of the mat is constant with fluidity, each movement is initiated through the powerhouse with control, the movements should be graceful and fluid with a dynamic energy, not rushed or jerky.

THE 4 KEY ELEMENTS TO A PILATES WORKOUT

The Powerhouse

Each exercise in the Pilates method involves your powerhouse. This is the band of muscle bound by the 'transversus abdominus' that is two inches below the navel and wraps around the torso. This also includes the hips, bottom, inner and outer thighs.

The powerhouse

Position of the Neck

The correct position whilst doing the mat is to keep the neck long and lengthened. Try not to lift the chin towards the ceiling, as this places strain on the neck muscles. During the mat, use your powerhouse to draw the chin to the chest – eyeline looking towards the navel. This will stretch and strengthen the muscles at the back of the neck. If you have a weak neck, place your head on a cushion for support.

Breathing

In Pilates, we inhale through the nose and exhale through the mouth. As you inhale, think of expanding the back on the mat. As you exhale, think of drawing the ribs together and 'scooping' i.e. drawing the navel to the spine.

Pilates Stance

In the authentic Pilates mat, we work in Pilates Stance – heels together and the toes slightly turned out into a 'v' position. The feeling is of wrapping the thighs around the legs, squeeze the bottom and the back of the inner thighs so the muscles in the front of the legs, the quadriceps, are relaxed.

THE HUNDRED

THE BASIC MODIFIED MAT

Breathing exercise that warms up the body and increases circulation.

1   Lie on your back, scoop in the belly, draw the knees to the chest, inhale. As you exhale, pull the knees in and press the tailbone to the mat.

2   Extend knees out over your hips, shins parallel with the floor. Reach the arms long from the armpits about 15cm–20cm off the floor and ensure your back is flat on the mat.

3   Using your powerhouse, bring chin to chest, press shoulders down into your back, and begin to pump arms.
    Inhale through the nose for 5 counts, exhale through the mouth for 5 counts, drawing your navel into the spine.

4   Try to reach 50. If you feel you are straining your neck, rest your head on a pillow. Gradually build up to 100.

5   Once you have reached your goal, draw knees to chest and rest the head.

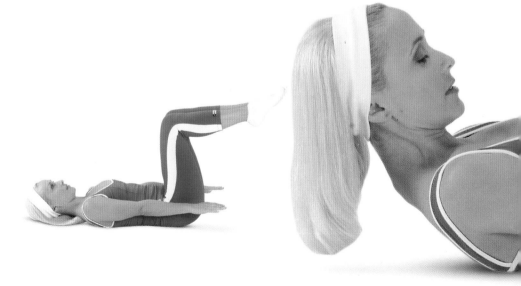

MODIFICATIONS

Neck: Place a small towel or pillow under your neck during exercise, so there is no strain on the neck, or so that the head can be placed down at any time. Begin by lifting your head firstly for 20 counts and then gradually, as neck becomes stronger, keep it lifted for 100 counts.

Lower Back: (disc problems, sciatica) keep knees bent so shins remain parallel to the floor.

Reach through the fingertips from armpits. Scoop in the navel, watch it sink down to the spine on the exhale.

If your neck is straining, put it down onto the pillow. Make sure the back is not arching. Try not to push the abdominals out as you breathe.

THE ROLL UP

THE BASIC MODIFIED MAT

Strengthens the powerhouse, articulates the spine and stretches the hamstrings.

MODIFICATION 1

1 Sitting upright, knees and feet hip width apart, hands holding onto back of thigh.

2 Drawing chin to chest, inhale. As you exhale, draw navel to spine and slightly tuck tailbone under as you roll down, trying to peel the first 4 vertebrae onto the mat.

3 Once the arms are almost straight, inhale, draw the navel deeper to the spine. Exhale, keep scooping in and come forward. Repeat 4 more times.

✓ Keep scooping in as you reach forward to your toes. Walk up and down your legs to help you scoop in the tummy. Keep squeezing the thighs together.

✗ Try not to let your feet come off the floor as you roll up and down. Try not to push your stomach out as you exhale.

MODIFICATION 2

1 Lie on your back, knees bent, inner thighs squeezed together, reaching the arms over head, make sure the whole spine is connected to the mat.

2 Lift the arms to the ceiling, draw your chin to your chest as if you were looking through the window the arms have created, inhale, scoop in the powerhouse and peel the spine off the mat (walk hands up the legs if you need assistance).

3 Exhale, as you lift up and over. Straightening the legs, make sure you are drawing navel to spine to acheive that oppositional pull. Feel the stretch in the hamstrings.

4 Inhale, start to peel your spine back onto the mat (walk down the legs until you are strong enough not to hold on). Drawing navel to spine, exhale as you reach the arms over your head and repeat 4 more times.

SINGLE LEG CIRCLES

THE BASIC MODIFIED MAT

Stretches and strengthens the leg in the hip joint,
stabilises the pelvis.

1 Lie on your back, palms down, bend your underneath leg,
   so your back is flat to the mat.

2 Lift your right leg to the ceiling, hold behind the thigh, calf or
   ankle, depending on your flexibility. Think of bringing the leg
   to the nose.

3 Place your hands by your side with the palms down, rotate the
   leg and reach across your body, first drawing a circle on the
   ceiling and then back up to the nose. Repeat 5 times and then
   reverse the circle 5 times. Finish each circle opposite the nose.

4 Try to keep your hips anchored to the mat, with as little
   movement as possible. Start with a small circle. As you get
   stronger, draw a bigger circle.

MODIFICATIONS

Lower Back Problems: Keep the underneath leg bent, so back stays flat to mat.

Tight Hamstrings: Keep the underneath leg bent.

Bad Hips: Leave this exercise out.

Think of wrapping your thigh around the leg, so you are working from the hip. Try to relax your quadricep muscle and work from the bottom.

Keep your toe pointing to the ceiling, so the leg doesn't drop and your back doesn't arch off the mat. Try not to turn the leg in. Try to lead with the inside of the heel.

Rolling Like A Ball

The Basic Modified Mat

Works the stomach, acts as a spinal massage for balance and control.

1 Sitting up, bend your knees into your chest, keeping the knees slightly apart and feet together. Place hands underneath the thighs (not behind the knee) and draw your heels into your bottom.

2 Bend the head forward, with the chin touching the chest, looking down to the navel. Draw your toes off the mat and balance on your sit bones.

3 Inhale, drawing your navel to your spine and roll backward, taking the legs with you. Try to keep the chin to your chest.

4 Exhale, scoop in deeper and come forward, maintaining the ball position. Repeat 5 more times.

Only roll up to the base of the shoulder blades. Use your powerhouse to initiate the roll back, by scooping in. Keep a good momentum on the rolling.

Try to keep your chin to your chest as you roll and not initiate the movement by throwing the head back. Do not close your eyes, as it inhibits your balance. Keep the feet as close to the bottom as possible. Try not to let them kick up.

SINGLE LEG STRETCH

THE BASIC MODIFIED MAT

Strengthens, works the powerhouse, stretches the back of the legs.

1 After the ball, roll back down to the mat and pull the right knee to your chest.

2 Place your left hand on the knee and right hand on the ankle (always think of your outside arm reaching to your ankle).

3 Draw chin to chest and extend the left leg high to the ceiling. Inhale, switch legs and arms simultaneously, then exhale when you change again. This is one set.

4 Repeat 5 more sets. Focus on scooping navel to spine to keep your back flat!

MODIFICATIONS

Lower Back Pain: Keep the legs above 45° angle.

Neck Pain: Keep the head on a pillow, gradually increase the length of time the head is held up.

Knee Pain: Hold the back of the thigh.

✓ Draw your knee into the chest as far as possible. Stretch the extended leg out of the hip.

✗ If you feel any strain in your neck, place your head down. If you feel the back arch, extend the leg higher to the ceiling.

DOUBLE LEG STRETCH

THE BASIC MODIFIED MAT

Strengthens and works the powerhouse, stretches the arms and the legs.

1 Lie flat, draw knees to chest. Draw chin to chest and hold
the ankles.

2 Inhale. Simultaneously extend arms to the ears and legs to
the ceiling.

3 Scoop navel to spine, exhale and circle the arms around and draw
the knees into the chest.

4 Repeat 5 more times.

MODIFICATIONS

Neck Pain: Keep the head down.
Knee Pain: Hold the back of thigh (as in previous exercise).
Lower Back: Keep the legs high.
Tight Hamstrings: Keep the knees soft on extension.

✓ As you extend the legs, wrap the thighs in Pilates stance. This is a breathing exercise, on the exhale, emphasise the 'scoop'.

✗ Don't take the arms behind the ears; it strains the neck. If you feel the back arch, lift your legs higher to the ceiling.

SPINE STRETCH
FORWARD

THE BASIC MODIFIED MAT

Stretches the hamstrings, opens the lower back and articulates the spine.

1 Sit as tall as possible, legs shoulder width apart, bend your knees slightly to release hamstrings.

2 Extend arms at shoulder height. Draw chin to chest, inhale and lift tall in the powerhouse.

3 Roll down through the spine, drawing the crown of the head towards the navel. Exhale, reaching forward whilst maintaining the c-curve.

4 Inhale. Scoop in deeper and stack the spine, vertebra per vertebra, until you're seated tall on your sit bones. Exhale. Repeat 3 more times.

✔ Maintain the c-curve throughout the exercise to open the lower back. Breathing is the key to a good stretch. Don't hold the breath.

✘ Don't let the knees roll inward as you stretch forward. Don't flop forward as you stretch. As you roll up, try not to lean back. Keep shoulders over hips and lengthen from the crown of the head.

THE HUNDRED

THE BASIC/INTERMEDIATE MAT

Breathing exercise, warm-up for body, increase circulation.

1 Lie on your back. Scoop in your belly, draw the knees into your chest. Draw the chin into your chest and reach the arms forward 15cm–20cm off the floor. Extend your legs up to the ceiling in Pilates stance and lower gradually, until you feel your powerhouse engage.

2 Pump the arms as if slapping water. Inhale through the nose for 5 counts and exhale through the mouth for 5 counts, scooping navel to spine.

3 Repeat until you reach 100.

On the exhale, make sure you really scoop navel to spine 'in and up' and keep reaching long with the arms to pull shoulders away from ears. Remember to squeeze the bottom and the back of the upper inner thighs to provide support for the lower back.

If you feel any back pain, lift the legs higher to the ceiling or bend the knees. Any neck pain, rest the head. Don't let the head drop back. Keep the chin glued to the chest.

THE ROLL UP

THE BASIC/INTERMEDIATE MAT

Strengthens the powerhouse, articulates the spine and stretches the hamstrings.

1 Lie flat on your back. Reach your arms back over your head to where your back is flat, extend the legs forward and together. (If your back is arching, bend your knees.) Draw the navel to the spine.

2 Inhaling, slowly reach your arms to the ceiling. Draw your chin to your chest. Start to peel your spine off the mat (walk the hands up the legs, if you are not quite strong enough to roll up).

3 As you roll up off the mat, keep the arms at shoulder height. Exhale as you continue forward, until the upper body is over the legs.

4 As you reach forward over the legs, think of lifting up out of the hips. Remember to keep drawing navel to spine to get the oppositional pull. Repeat 4 more times.

Think of rolling up like a carpet,
really scooping in and stretching the
body as you reach forward. Try to
keep the 'flow' as you roll up and
back down to the mat.

To ensure you are using the muscles
of the powerhouse, do not roll up
using your neck and shoulders. Press
the shoulders away from the ears.
Press the back of the thighs down
onto the mat. Try not to let the legs
lift as you roll up.

SINGLE LEG CIRCLES

THE BASIC/INTERMEDIATE MAT

Stretches and strengthens the leg in the hip joint and stabilises the pelvis.

1 Lie on your back, palms down. Extend the left leg to the ceiling, keeping the underneath leg straight. Hold behind your thigh, calf or ankle and gently stretch the hamstring.

2 Palms down, place the hands to the mat, scoop in navel to spine and reach into your fingertips, pulling the shoulders down into the back.

3 Rotate the leg and reach across the body, draw a circle on the ceiling and back up to the nose. The circle can be a little bigger now, as long as your hips are stabilised. Do 5 circles then reverse in the opposite direction 5 times.

4 Remember, scoop in navel to spine to anchor the spine to the mat and to keep the hips as still as possible.

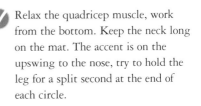

Relax the quadricep muscle, work from the bottom. Keep the neck long on the mat. The accent is on the upswing to the nose, try to hold the leg for a split second at the end of each circle.

Do not arch the back off the mat. If the hip clicks or pops, keep the range of motion small.

ROLLING LIKE A BALL

THE BASIC/INTERMEDIATE MAT

Works the powerhouse, massages the spine for balance and control.

1 Sit at the front edge of your mat. Bend your knees into the chest and hold your ankles. Draw the chin towards the chest and try to draw the ears as close to the knees as possible, so you are round like a ball.

2 Draw your toes off the mat and balance. Keep the legs in a 'v' shape, feet together, knees shoulder width apart.

3 Draw the navel deep into your spine, so much that it draws you back onto the mat, inhaling.

4 Exhale, scoop in deeper and roll forward, balancing on your sit bones and keeping the head tucked. Repeat 5 more times.

Inhale to roll back, exhale to roll forward, scoop in as deep as you can to use the powerhouse to come up. Keep the heels as close to the bottom as possible.

Do not initiate the roll by throwing your head back. As you roll forward, try to not push forward with your back to come up. Don't let the feet kick up over the head as you roll back.

SINGLE LEG STRETCH

THE BASIC/INTERMEDIATE MAT

The first exercise of five that make up the 'Stomach Series' – strengthens the powerhouse.

1 As you finish the last roll of the ball, balance. Slide back on your mat and draw the right knee to your chest, left hand on your knee and the right hand on your ankle.

2 Inhale and switch hands and legs. Keep reaching the underneath leg to the opposite side of the room. Exhale and switch hands and legs again. Repeat 5 more sets.

MODIFICATIONS

Lower Back Pain: Keep the legs at 45°.

Neck Pain: Try to keep the head up for half the exercise and down for half, until your neck gets stronger.

Knee Pain: Hold under the knee.

✓ Keep your chin glued to your chest. As you switch legs, keep scooping your navel to your spine. Keep the elbows lifted to work the back of the arms and press the shoulders away from the ears.

✗ Keep the extended leg at a height so you don't let the back arch off the mat. If there is any strain on the neck, place the head down onto a cushion.

DOUBLE LEG STRETCH

THE BASIC/INTERMEDIATE MAT

The second exercise of the 'Stomach Series' – works the powerhouse, stretches the body.

1 Lie flat, draw knees to chest. Draw the chin to the chest and hold the ankles.

2 Inhale. Reach arms to the ears, extend legs forward at a 45° angle. Wrap the legs in Pilates stance.

3 Scoop navel to spine, exhale and circle the arms around and draw the knees into the chest. Repeat 6–8 times.

As you reach into the position, think of lengthening through the waist. When the legs are extended, squeeze the back of the inner thighs to hold the legs in Pilates stance.

On the exhale, scoop in the belly.

Keep scooping navel to spine, don't let the back arch off the mat. To stop the neck from straining, keep the chin on the chest.

SINGLE LEG STRAIGHT

THE BASIC/INTERMEDIATE MAT

The third exercise of the 'Stomach Series' – stretches the hamstrings, works the powerhouse.

1 Extend both legs to the ceiling, chin to chest.
Make sure the base of your shoulder blades stay on the mat.

2 Place both hands on right leg. Depending on flexibility, hold back of thigh, calf or ankle (not the back of the knee).

3 Lower left leg down about 45° off the mat or until your back is flat.

4 Draw shoulders down into the back, elbows to the side. Inhale.
Pull the 'up leg' with a double pulse towards you, in a
scissor-like action. Switch legs, keeping them straight.
Exhale. Repeat the double pulse on the other leg.
Repeat 6–8 more times.

Keep a nice rhythm in this exercise.
Try to use the powerhouse to pulse
the leg, not the arms. Really scoop
in as you scissor the legs and keep
them straight.

Do not let the shoulders lift too high
off the mat. Do not use the arms to
pulse the leg. If the stretch is too
intense, hold the thigh at first.

DOUBLE LEG STRAIGHT

THE BASIC/INTERMEDIATE MAT

The fourth (and hardest) exercise of the 'Stomach Series' – strengthens upper and lower powerhouse, works the back of the legs.

MODIFICATION 1

1 Place one hand on top of the other, chin to chest, bend legs, shins parallel to floor.

2 Inhale. Draw the toes down towards the mat, make sure the back does not arch.

3 Scoop in the powerhouse. Exhale. Keep scooping in deeper, draw legs back up to where they started. Repeat 5 times.

MODIFICATION 2

1 Place one hand on top of the other, chin to chest, legs extended to ceiling. Wrap the thighs.

2 Inhale. Squeeze the back of the inner thighs together and lower the legs, only as far as you can. Maintain a flat back.

3 Exhale. Scoop in deeper and bring the legs up to the start position. Repeat 5 times.

✓ Keep the chin to the chest, use the powerhouse to draw the legs up, not the hip flexors.

✓ Scoop the navel in and up to start with. Only lower the legs as far as you can keep the back flat. Pilates stance, squeeze the back of the legs.

✗ Do not let the back arch off the mat. Keep the range of motion small at first, until you get stronger.

✗ Do not let the head/shoulders lower as the legs lower.

CRISS CROSS

THE BASIC/INTERMEDIATE MAT

The fifth and last exercise in the 'Stomach Series' – works the powerhouse, external oblique and waistline and upper back.

1 Chin to chest, knees to chest, fingertips lightly touching back of head, keep the elbows open.

2 Extend the left leg out at a 45° angle. Inhale. Lift and twist your upper body until the left elbow comes to the right knee. Exhale. Look back towards the right elbow, keep the underneath shoulder off the mat and hold.

3 Inhale. Switch legs and bring the right elbow to the left knee and look back as you exhale. Look towards the left elbow. Keep lifting the shoulders off the mat. Repeat 1 more time.

MODIFICATIONS

Lower Back Pain: (Herniated discs or lower back pain). Leave this exercise out, as the spine doesn't like to rotate.

Delicate Neck: Leave out at first. As you get stronger, add in.

✓ Maintain the c-curve throughout to open the lower back. Breathing is the key to a good stretch. Don't hold the breath.

✗ Remember to keep shoulders over the hip bones and press them down from the ears.

SPINE STRETCH FORWARD

THE BASIC/INTERMEDIATE MAT

Stretches the hamstrings, opens and articulates the spine.

1 Sit as tall as possible, legs shoulder width apart, and reach through the heels.

2 Extend the arms at shoulder height and draw chin to chest, inhale and lift tall in the powerhouse.

3 Roll down through the spine, drawing the crown of the head towards the navel. Exhale, and reach forward whilst maintaining the c-curve.

4 Inhale, scoop in deeper and stack the spine vertebra per vertebra to your tall seated position, lifting in the powerhouse. Exhale. Repeat 3 more times.

✓ Maintain the c-curve throughout to open the lower back. Breathing is the key to a good stretch. Don't hold the breath.

✗ Remember to keep shoulders over the hip bones and press them down from the ears.

OPEN LEG ROCKER

THE BASIC/INTERMEDIATE MAT

Massages the spine, stretches the hamstring, opens the lower back, works balance and control.

1 Sit forward at the edge of your mat. Place thumb and forefinger over the ankles, with arms on the inside of the thighs (to open the lower back), keep knees the width of your shoulders to stay in your box.

2 Scoop into your powerhouse, draw heels into your bottom and balance on your sit bones. Extend right leg. Scoop in the belly and lift tall in the lower back, lower leg and repeat on the left leg, then simultaneously straighten both legs and balance.

3 Drop chin to chest. Inhale. Scoop in the belly. Exhale and roll back only up to your shoulder blades. Keep the arms and legs straight.

4 Inhale as you roll back up onto the sit bones, lift tall from the crown of your head and scoop in the powerhouse. Repeat 5 more times.

✔ Increase flexibility in the hamstrings. Scoop in navel to spine to initiate the rolling back.

✘ Do not throw your head back to initiate the rolling. Do not roll past your upper back or onto your neck. Do not sit into your lower back, keep lifted in the powerhouse.

CORKSCREW

THE BASIC/INTERMEDIATE MAT

Works your powerhouse, stretches the hamstrings, stretches your back and improves balance.

1 Lie back down onto the mat and extend the body out. Keep the neck long, push into the palm of your hands and extend the legs to the ceiling, wrapping the thighs.

2 Inhale, begin to make a small circle to the right, drawing the navel to spine.

3 Exhale. Scoop the belly in deeper. Draw the legs to the centre.

4 Repeat, this time moving the legs to the left. Repeat 3 sets, alternating right to left.

MODIFICATIONS

Tight Hamstrings: Keep the knees bent but legs together, place your thumbs and forefingers together and under your tailbone to keep the feet over the hips.

Lower Back: Ensure the back stays flat. Keep the range of motion really small.

✓ Emphasise scooping navel to spine to keep the back flat. Relax the neck, shoulders and back throughout the exercise. Start with a small circle. As your powerhouse gets stronger, draw a bigger circle.

✗ If you feel any back pain, draw a smaller circle to reduce the range of motion.

NECK PULL

THE BASIC/INTERMEDIATE MAT

Works the powerhouse, stretches the hamstrings and lengthens/articulates the spine.

1 Lie flat on your back with the legs hip width apart, either bent or straight. Place the hands behind the head one on top of the other.

2 Inhale. Lift the chin to the chest. Lift up as high as you can, make sure you are scooping in and then walk the hands up the back of the legs, or keep the hands behind the head and roll up.

3 Scoop in the belly as you round over, exhale stretching the back and the neck. (Imagine rounding over a big beach ball). Inhale. Scoop in deeper and slowly roll up, stacking the spine vertebra per vertebra.

4 Chin to chest, scoop in, exhale, lengthen the spine and slowly peel down onto the mat, vertebra per vertebra. Press the first 4 vertebrae into the mat as you roll. To control the roll down, walk the hands down the legs, bending the knees if you need to. No crashing! Repeat 4 more times.

MODIFIED

Keep the elbows out to the sides of
the room. Initiate the movement
from the powerhouse.

If your feet are lifting while rolling,
either bend the knees or tuck the feet
under the couch for resistance or have
someone hold them. Try to touch the
first 4 vertebrae onto the mat first
when rolling down.

INTERMEDIATE

THE SIDE KICK SERIES

THE BASIC/INTERMEDIATE MAT

1. FORWARD AND BACK

Works inner/outer thigh, strengthens glutes, increases flexibility. Excellent for finding balance and works symmetry.

1 Lay on the back edge of your mat, elbow in line with the hip, hips in line with the feet and then bring the feet forward to a 45° angle. Place the other hand on the mat directly in front of ribs. Press firmly into palm of hand to stabilise the torso.

2 Lift your top leg to hip height and rotate the leg outwards from the hip, so the knee points towards the ceiling.

3 Inhale. Draw your navel into your spine and stretch your leg to the front with a double pulse. Try to keep the torso stable and the hips stacked one on top of the other.

4 As you stretch your leg back, exhale and scoop in deeper to ensure minimal movement in the torso.

5 Repeat 9 more times. On the last one bring the heels together to prepare for up/down kick.

(Applies to all side kick series.)
Elbows/wrists/shoulder/neck:
Lay with a flat arm, head on a small pillow.
Lower Back/Sciatic Pain:
Keep range of motion smaller.
For Men: Only do sidekick forward and back.

✓ Try to keep torso stable, long and lengthened throughout these exercises. Remember to keep hips stacked.

✗ Don't let the leg drop below hip height. If you feel unstable, reduce the range of motion until you are stronger. Try to work from the hip as you reach forward – do not kick from the knee.

2. UP/DOWN

Works the inner and outer thigh, glutes and hips.

1 You have just completed your forward and back – stay in the same position. Lift your leg to hip height, slightly rotated from the hip, so knee points towards the ceiling. The foot is relaxed.

2 Inhale to lift the leg without rocking back in the hips (as you become more flexible, the range of motion will increase).

3 Exhale. Reach your leg long out of your hip and resist on the way back down. (Imagine you're trying to burst a balloon between your inner thighs on the way down.) Repeat 4 more times and bring the heels together to prepare for the small circles.

THE SIDE KICK SERIES

(CONTINUED)

3. SMALL CIRCLES

Works the inner and outer thigh, glutes and hips.

1 You have just completed your up/down. Lying in the same position, rotate the top leg to hip height, keeping the hips stacked.

2 Begin to circle the leg 5 times to the front and 5 times in the opposite direction. Try to keep the circles the size of a bread and butter plate!

3 Try to squeeze your inner thighs together as you circle your leg from your hip and maintain the squeezing of your bottom.

4 To finish, lower the heels together and roll onto your stomach for your transition to the other side.

After completing the 'Side Kick' series, you should feel a 'worked' sensation through the outer thigh.

If you only felt the work in the quadriceps, then work on rotating the leg from the hip and relax the quadricep.

TRANSITION HEEL BEATS

Works the back of the thighs and the bottom.

1   Lay on your stomach, place one hand on top of the other, elbows to the side, forehead resting on top of the hands.

2   Draw navel to spine, squeeze the inner thighs together and your bottom and lift the legs off the mat. Keep the legs straight, heels together.

3   Beat the heels together 10 times. Think about resisting the inner thighs and really scoop in your tummy. If you have a weak lower back, continue here for another 10 beats. If not go to step 4.

4   For a slightly harder variation, lift your legs slightly higher. Keep scooping in, squeezing the bottom and inner thighs and beat for a further 10 beats.

5   Lay on your other side to complete the side kick series on the other leg.

Teaser Preparation 1

THE BASIC/INTERMEDIATE MAT

Strengthens the powerhouse, promotes balance and control.

1 Lie on your back with your legs bent and together, squeezing through the bottom and inner thighs. Extend the arms over the head (palms face up) to where your back is flat, drawing your navel to spine.

2 To keep the flow, inhale, reach the arms to the ceiling, lift chin to chest, scoop in and roll up into a c-curve position, exhaling. (Draw the shoulders down into the back, look up to your fingertips.)

3 Inhale. Chin to chest, scoop in deeper and peel the spine down to the mat, pressing the feet into the floor, squeezing the inner thighs and the bottom.

4 As you roll down and the head touches the mat, exhale and reach the arms back behind you. Repeat twice.

MODIFICATIONS

Lower Back Problems:
Ensure back is flat and keep the arms high.

✓ As you roll up, keep lifted in the powerhouse. Remember to squeeze inner thighs and bottom throughout exercise.

✕ If you feel your back arching, press the first 4 vertebrae into the mat as you roll down. If you have trouble rolling up, walk up the back of the legs a little until you are strong enough in your powerhouse to roll up.

THE SEAL

THE BASIC/INTERMEDIATE MAT

Cool-down exercise, massages the spine, works the powerhouse, promotes balance and control.

1 Sit at the end of the mat. Bring the feet together (soles touching), separate the knees shoulder width apart and place the hands inside the legs and hold onto the sides of the ankles.

2 Draw the navel to the spine and drop the chin to the chest. Lift the feet off the mat and balance. You should be carving a c-curve with your torso. Clap the feet together 3 times. Inhale and initiate the rolling back from the powerhouse.

3 Roll only onto the shoulder blades of the upper back. NOT ON YOUR NECK! Control your rolling and clap the feet another 3 times over your head. Scoop in deeper. Exhale and roll back up.

4 Hold your balance on your sit bones at the end of each roll, scooping in, clap the feet again and roll 5 more times.

Modifications

Shoulder/Elbow Problems:
Leave this exercise out.

Weak Lower Back/Bad Back/Neck Problems:
Leave this exercise out.

 This is a cool down – your final mat exercise. Enjoy the massage on the spine.

Try not to initiate the roll by throwing back the head. Make sure you control the rolling – don't roll onto the neck!

THE WALL

ARM CIRCLES ON THE WALL

This is your cool down. Great for alignment and to stretch and lengthen the spine. This sequence will complete your workout. It will ensure your posture will be upright and the body balanced for the rest of the day. Can be done with weights for extra stretch.

1 Stand against the wall in Pilates stance. Walk your feet forward until you feel the full length of your spine against the wall. The knees should be soft and make sure you are pressing your navel to your spine. Press your shoulders down into your back and open across the chest. Use light weights for added benefit during this exercise.

2 Inhale as you lift your arms to shoulder height.

3 Open your arms and lengthen across the chest.

4 Exhale. Keep scooping navel to spine and lower the arms down. Repeat twice and then reverse in opposite direction. Once completed, keep arms by the side to prepare for sliding down the wall.

Keep elbows soft and arms relaxed.

 Don't let back arch off wall.
Keep scooping in.

SLIDING DOWN
THE WALL

1   You have just completed the arm
    circles. Turn your feet parallel, hip
    width apart. Depending on your
    height, take your feet out further
    from the wall.

2   Inhale. Bend your knees and raise
    your arms to shoulder height as you
    slide your back down the wall.

3   Do not take your bottom below your
    knees. Try to maintain a right angle
    in the legs. Scoop in to keep the
    back flat.

4   Exhale. Lower the arms, resisting like
    you are pressing a great weight down.
    Scoop in deeper and slide back up
    the wall.

5   Draw your heels into Pilates stance to
    prepare for rolling down the wall.

ROLLING DOWN
THE WALL

1   Inhale. Draw your chin to your chest.
    Scoop in the powerhouse and press
    your lower back into the wall.

2   Peel your spine off the wall vertebra
    per vertebra, exhaling and keeping
    the arms relaxed, roll down to where
    the tailbone stays in contact with the
    wall. (Any disc problems, keep range
    of motion smaller and only roll as far
    as you feel comfortable.)

3   With relaxed arms, circle 5 times one
    way and then reverse in the opposite
    direction. Keep drawing navel to spine.

4   Inhale, scoop in and peel the spine
    back up the wall, vertebra per
    vertebra. The head is the last to unroll.

5   Place the palm of the hands back onto
    the wall. Keep lifting tall from the
    crown of the head, walk your heels
    back against the wall. Pull your
    shoulders down, scoop the navel
    in and up and press away from the
    wall and step forward.

BASIC MODIFIED MAT

EXERCISE	BENEFITS	COUNTS	
The Hundred	Breathing exercise, circulates the blood, warms the body.	Inhale 5 counts Exhale 5 counts 10 x	
The Roll-Up	Articulates the spine, strengthens the powerhouse, stretches the hamstrings.	5 x	
Single Leg Circles	Stretches the hamstrings, strengthens the leg in the hip joint, stabilises the pelvis from the powerhouse.	5 each way	
Rolling Like a Ball	Massages the spine, strengthens and works the powerhouse, promotes balance and control.	6 x	
Single Leg Stretch	First exercise of the stomach series. Strengthens the powerhouse, stretches the legs.	6 x	
Double Leg Stretch	Second exercise of the stomach series. Strengthens the powerhouse, stretches the legs.	6 x	
Spine Stretch Forward	Opens and articulates the spine, works the powerhouse, stretches the hamstrings.	4 x	

THE MODIFIED BASIC MAT

The Basics are essential to the 6 principles of the Pilates method (refer to pages 6 & 7).

By following the Basic Modified Mat, until you are strong enough in your powerhouse, you can then move onto the Basic Mat, which still includes the original exercises with a slightly harder progression.

Mastering these is essential, so that you can advance to the intermediate levels.

BASIC/INTERMEDIATE MAT

EXERCISE	BENEFITS	COUNTS	
BASIC MAT START WITH THE BASIC MAT			
	The Hundred	10 x	
	The Roll-Up	5 x	
	Single Leg Circles	5 each way	
	Rolling Like a Ball	6 x	
	Single Leg Stretch	6–8 x	
	Double Leg Stretch	6–8 x	
Single Leg Straight	Stretches the hamstrings, works the powerhouse.	6–8 x	
Double Leg Straight	Strengthens the upper and lower powerhouse, works the back of the legs	6–8 x	
Criss Cross	Works the powerhouse, external obliques, waistline and upper back.	2 x	
Spine Stretch Forward	Stretches the hamstrings, opens and articulates the spine.	4 x	
Open Leg Rocker	Massages the spine, stretches the hamstring, opens the lower back, works balance and control.	6 x	
Corkscrew	Works your powerhouse, stretches the hamstrings and the back, improves balance.	6 x	
Neck Pull	Works the powerhouse, stretches the hamstrings, lengthens and articulates the spine.	5 x	
Sidekicks: 1. Forward/Back	Works inner/outer thigh, strengthens the glutes, increases flexibility.	10 x	
2. Up/Down	Works inner/outer thighs, hips and glutes.	5 x	
3. Circles	Works the inner and outer thigh, glutes and hips.	5 x each way	
Teaser Prep 1.	Strengthens the powerhouse, promotes balance and control.	3 x	
Seal	Cool–down exercise, massages the spine, works the powerhouse, promotes balance and control.	6 x	

☐ Basic Mat   ☐ Basic/Intermediate Mat

CONCLUSION

The Pilates Method should continue to challenge you as it is a progressive form of exercise, so keep working towards your ultimate goal. Try NOT to add too many new exercises at once.

Remember to obtain the maximum benefit from your workout, always enforce the principles of stretch, strength and control, and you will be on your way to achieving a more balanced and healthy body.

GLOSSARY

TERMINOLOGY

Articulation

Peeling the spine segmentally down to the mat, as in the roll up.

Lengthening

Think of 'growing tall'. Imagine you are being pulled through the crown of the head like a puppet on a string and reach out and extend the body through the spine.

Powerhouse

The band of muscle about 4cm below the navel that wraps around the torso. The powerhouse region includes the inner and outer thighs, bottom and hips.

Pilates Stance

Heels together, toes splayed open to create a small 'v', wrapping the thighs around the legs and squeezing the back of the inner thighs together.

Navel to Spine

The feeling of pulling the navel deep down internally and anchoring the back down to the mat, as if there is a great weight pressing you down.

Scoop

The feeling of 'scooping' – drawing the navel in and up internally.

The Box

Two imaginary lines, one from shoulder to shoulder and the other from hip to hip.

MUSCLES

Triceps

The extensor muscle at the back of the arm.

Quadriceps

The muscles that run down the front of the thigh. With its four bodies acting together, the quadriceps extend the knee and is the strongest muscle in the body.

Hamstrings

The muscles that run from the top of the leg down and cross over behind the knee. A group of three posterior muscles working together to flex the knee and extend the thigh.

Gluteus Maximus

The largest muscle of the body, provides the bulk of the buttocks.

Tranversus Abdominus

The deepest of the four, contraction of these fibres reduces the circumference of the abdomen by 'pulling in the belly' or 'scooping'.

Internal Oblique

Causes compression of the abdomen and assists in flexion of the torso.

External Oblique

Contraction of the external oblique results in side-bending and rotation of the spine and ribcage.

Rectus Abdominals

This muscle is mainly a flexor of the torso, but also assists the other three in compressing the abdomen.

DINA MATTY (pictured left)

Dina is a trained dancer, aerobics champion and expert fitness teacher, who studied dance in England. An exciting career in professional dancing saw Dina on television and in videos all around the world. Taking up aerobics, Dina became the UK and European champion two years in a row. Passionate about the benefits of Pilates, Dina trained with the New York Pilates Studio in Sydney under Master teachers Romana Kryzanowska and Cynthia Lochard. She is dedicated to teaching Pilates in its original format. Now in Australia, she has settled on the Gold Coast in Queensland, where she has set up Pulse Health Studio in Broadbeach.

KEFT BURDELL (pictured right)

Keft studied drama, movement and film at Melbourne University with a Bachelor of Education Arts. She also studied dance in the forms of classical, modern and tap. Keft combined her professional experience into becoming a successful personal trainer. To specialise in the field of pilates, she then completed her training with the New York Pilates Studio in Sydney under Master trainers Romana Kryzanowska and Cynthia Lochard. They teach the Pilates Method originally developed by Joseph H Pilates. Keft now lives on the Gold Coast in Queensland and works alongside Dina at Pulse Health Studio.